THE DAY THE WORLD CHANGED

How should Christians respond to

11 September 2001?

R. T. KENDALL

Hodder & Stoughton
LONDON SYDNEY AUCKLAND

Copyright © 2001 R. T. Kendall

First published in Great Britain in 2001

The right of R. T. Kendall to be identified as the Author of
the Work has been asserted by him in accordance with
the Copyright, Designs and Patents Act 1988.

10 9 8 7 6 5 4 3 2 1

British Library Cataloguing in Publication Data
A record for this book is available from the British Library

ISBN 0 340 78711 2

Typeset by Avon Dataset Ltd, Bidford-on-Avon, Warks

Printed and bound in Great Britain by
Bookmarque Ltd, Croydon, Surrey

Hodder & Stoughton
A Division of Hodder Headline Ltd
338 Euston Road
London NW1 3BH

To Annette

CONTENTS

PREFACE

Like many of you, I remember exactly where I was on 22 November 1963, the day President John F. Kennedy was assassinated. And likewise, I remember exactly where I was when I received the shocking news of the attack on New York and Washington on 11 September 2001.

I had just come in from a few hours' fishing with Captain Harry Spears in Islamorada, Florida. We walked into our favourite restaurant and noticed the TV was on and the volume up. There were big letters – 'Attack on

America' – on the screen, but my immediate reaction was that this was a science fiction movie! Then I looked closer and noticed that it was CNN – live. My heart nearly stopped. I shouted at Harry: 'Come here quickly! This is big! This is awful!'

And so it was. It was the day the world changed. None of us could think about anything else for many days. I was stuck in Florida. I could not get a plane back to London for several days, and had time to reflect.

I cancelled the sermon I prepared for the first Sunday back at Westminster Chapel, and instead preached a sermon entitled 'The Day the World Changed'. It did not cross my mind that this would go into print, but it follows in this little book. It has been edited to make it read better.

A few days after that I was asked by Reverend Joel Edwards to speak briefly to an Evangelical Alliance prayer meeting at Westminster Chapel which had been scheduled for many months. The original purpose of the evening was to pray about crime in London, but because of the magnitude of recent events the prayer meeting was widened to include the whole international situation.

I gave a brief talk in which I called for 'a new kind of hero'. This message was apparently well-received and it would seem that it fits well with the sermon to which I have referred above.

I pray that this little book will have wide distribution. It can be used both evangelistically as well as to enlarge our vision. But if it will drive us to our knees, and produce a new kind of hero, all the better!

This book is lovingly dedicated to our daughter-in-law, Annette. She and T. R. are happily married and living in Florida.

R. T. Kendall
Westminster Chapel,
London
16 October 2001

1

THE DAY THE WORLD CHANGED

Then the angel I had seen standing on the sea and on the land raised his right hand to heaven. And he swore by him who lives for ever and ever, who created the heavens and all that is in them, the earth and all that is in it, and the sea and all that is in it, and said, 'There will be no more delay! But in the days when the seventh angel is about to sound his trumpet, the mystery of

God will be accomplished, just as he announced to his servants the prophets.'

Then the voice that I had heard from heaven spoke to me once more: 'Go, take the scroll that lies open in the hand of the angel who is standing on the sea and on the land.'

So I went to the angel and asked him to give me the little scroll. He said to me, 'Take it and eat it. It will turn your stomach sour, but in your mouth it will be as sweet as honey.' I took the little scroll from the angel's hand and ate it. It tasted as sweet as honey in my mouth, but when I had eaten it, my stomach turned sour. Then I was told, 'You must prophesy again about *many peoples, nations, languages and kings.'*

(Revelation 10:5–11)

'Therefore in one day her plagues will overtake her: death, mourning and famine. She will be consumed by fire, for mighty is the Lord God who judges her.'

(Revelation 18:8)

Terrified at her torment, they will stand far off and cry: 'Woe! Woe, O great city, O Babylon, city of power! In one hour your doom has come!'

(Revelation 18:10)

The merchants who sold these things and gained their wealth from her will stand far off, terrified at her torment. They will weep and mourn and cry out: 'Woe! Woe, O great city, dressed in fine linen, purple and scarlet, and glittering with gold, precious stones and pearls! In one hour such great wealth has been brought to ruin!' Every sea captain, and all who travel by ship, the sailors, and all who earn their living from the sea, will stand far off. When they see the smoke of her burning, they will exclaim, 'Was there ever a city like this great city?' They will throw dust on their heads, and with weeping and mourning cry out: 'Woe! Woe, O great city, where

all who had ships on the sea became
rich through her wealth! In one hour
she has been brought to ruin!'
                    (Revelation 18:15–19)

Be still, my soul: thy God doth undertake
To guide the future as He has the past,
Thy hope, thy confidence, let nothing shake;
All now mysterious shall be bright at last.

KATHERINE VON SCHLEGEL, B. 1697;
TR. JANE LAURIE BORTHWICK, 1813–97

Heavenly Father, we believe the words of
this hymn. We don't understand all that has
happened in recent days and you don't intend
for us to know everything. But we know

enough to know that you have allowed it. For all I know, you purposed it and caused it. And it's at times like this we prove what we really believe. For faith to be faith, it has to remain full of trust even though there is no good rational explanation to be had by looking at things. Why we should keep on believing, Lord? You have given us a splendid opportunity to show that we *do* believe. Can we say with Job, 'Though he slay me, yet will I trust him'?

And so we would like for all the angels to bear witness, that when we affirm you, we worship you. We love you. We affirm you for being God just as your word describes. And what is more, we love you for being just like you are. We affirm your sovereignty, your power, your honour and your glory. We affirm the Bible, your word. And we are going to trust you more than ever.

We pray that it might please you to give us a measure of understanding that we can, to the degree that it honours you, make sense of recent events. We pray that we will be renewed with confidence, but perhaps sobered. We pray above all to be more determined to bring great honour and glory to your name. So grant, O Lord, that the word to follow will please you. And if it be possible, that I will reflect word for word just what you want said. If I say something that could be in the flesh, unguarded, or ill-posed, that it will be forgotten and cleansed by your blood. But the degree to which I speak exactly what you want said, O Lord, apply this by your Spirit, that we are hemmed in and have no choice but to take your word on board.

We pause now to pray for those who suffer. Even as we are worshipping you, there are those in hospitals in pain. We think of those who grieve. Thousands and thousands who still do not know for sure whether that personal loved one is alive. We pray that you will comfort them. We pray for those also who are from the Middle East, and who are looked upon with suspicion, but who are totally innocent. We think of the family of the Sikh Indian in Arizona who, just because of the colour of his skin, was shot in his shop. Even if he had been an Arab, it would not have been justified. We pray for Arabs, for Jews, and for those of all colours who know what it is to be the object of racial prejudice. We bless them and comfort them.

We pray for those who make decisions and are making them now. And we pray that you will give to those in positions of authority, cool heads, warm hearts. That they will not be motivated by vengeance or hate, but by wisdom. And so we pray for President Bush, and for Tony Blair. We think of other heads of state and we thank you for the way our two nations in particular, often referred to as having a special relationship, are finding it more special than ever. But grant us your overruling guidance and clear wisdom. Grant that we will pray for our leaders and not be disillusioned or impatient if mistakes are made. We pray for all Muslims who are in fear, and feel that they will be judged. Hasten the day when the blindness which is upon Israel and the Islamic world will be lifted, that we may see your glory in these very last days. We pray for your word being preached wherever that is happening, in London, across the Atlantic, and around the world. We pray for the flourishing of the gospel. We pray for peace in the Middle East, and for the peace of Jerusalem. We pray for the people of Afghanistan, and for your mercy upon all those countries affected by the recent crisis. We pray for a permanent peace in Northern Ireland. God bless the United Kingdom and protect our cities. God bless America. God save the Queen. All these things we pray in Jesus' name. Amen.

On 11 September 2001, what is being called America's 'second Pearl Harbour' marked what I personally believe will turn out to be the beginning of the end so far as events that lead to the second coming of Jesus are concerned. The events of 7 December 1941 and 11 September 2001 not only brought Britain and America closer together, but changed the world.

We are now in a new kind of war. When the two planes hit each of the twin towers of the World Trade Centre in New York City and another landed on the Pentagon, a new era of terrorism was suddenly ushered in.

No one is safe any more. People who travel, people who go to work. People who are walking down the street with their families. Not even the perpetrators are safe any more because they have made themselves targets for as long as they live. No one can be sure of their financial situation any more. People have lost their jobs. Those who have their jobs aren't sure they will have them tomorrow. Financial institutions could lose everything overnight. All of us have been affected by this.

There is something symbolic about the twin towers in New York City. They symbolise secularism, the glory of humankind, capitalism, individuality, self-centredness. In one hour they came down, both within one hour. 'Woe! Woe, O great city, in one hour your doom has come.' If some prophet had said a year before that the twin towers of New York City would come down because of knives and box-cutters, no one would have believed them. But did not Isaiah see it long ago: 'In the day of great slaughter, when the towers fall . . .' (Isaiah 30:25)?

No one is secure any more. Our families are not secure, nor are our friends. I have to tell you terrorism – worse than anything that we have yet seen – is here to stay. Nothing is sacrosanct any more. The Pope, the Queen, the Prime Minister, children, Big Ben, Buckingham Palace, St Paul's. What has been called 'a new kind of evil' will not regard anything or anybody with any respect.

Nothing is shocking any more. Nothing will surprise us now, whether it be a hijacking or the use of chemical weapons. The depth to which some now reach, to destroy anything that is good in the earth, now knows no limits.

So we are talking about a day when the world changed, with particular reference to our perspective. It will never be the same again. Life as we have known it will be different. Speaking to a joint session of Congress with Tony Blair as the special guest, President George W. Bush could only forecast that the day would come when things would be 'almost' normal, but never the same. And we wonder if it will ever be almost normal at some stage. I doubt it.

Has all of this taken God by surprise? Well, there are things described in the book of Revelation that promise worse yet. We need to realise that.

Generally speaking, in the Church for a number of years there have been two opposite eschatological views. Eschatology refers to last days, the end times, in prophecy. One view is that the world will get worse and worse and this is the most you can expect. There is another view that revival will come that will be greater than Pentecost – the church revived and many converted, Jews being converted, many Islamic people turning to the Lord.

I believe that both views are equally true. The present evil will ultimately serve to bring us to great revival but also great persecution. 'In the day of great slaughter, when the towers fall, streams of water will flow on every high mountain and every lofty hill' (Isaiah 30:25). That suggests revival in parallel with tribulation. And the ways of humankind will wax worse and worse. Many will be saved but not all. It was never promised that everybody would be saved. Not all were saved as a result of Pentecost. Not all will be saved in the coming revival. But then Jesus will come.

The events of 11 September 2001 have shaken the world rigid. Yes, it has been called 'a new kind of evil', but is it new? Can we make sense of this event? A big question is, where does total forgiveness come in? How do we apply the teachings of Jesus? For example, at a time like this do we really believe the words of Jesus – 'Love your neighbour'?

You have heard that it was said, 'Love your neighbour and hate your enemy.' But I tell you: Love your enemies and pray for those who persecute you, that you may be sons of your Father in heaven. He causes his sun to rise on the evil and the good, and sends rain on the righteous and the unrighteous. If you love those who love you, what reward will you get? Are not even the

*tax collectors doing that? And if you
greet only your brothers, what are you
doing more than others? Do not even
pagans do that? Be perfect, therefore,
as your heavenly Father is perfect.*
(Matthew 5:43–8)

There are four issues I must address. First,
why did God allow this? I was pleased to hear
that at least one of the murdered pilots of the
plane that hit the World Trade Centre was a
Christian. Fine, but what about his family?
What about their grief? And what about those
who died but who were not saved? Why did
God allow this? The broader issue is: Why
does God allow evil? There is no answer to
that, this side of heaven. The closest we get to

the answer to the question, 'Why does God allow evil' is: in order that we might believe.

Let me explain. It's easy for a person to believe in God if they say, 'Lord, let me win the lottery . . .' and that day they win. They say, 'I believe in God.' It's easy to believe in God when you are promised prosperity and you also prosper. You then say, 'I believe in God.' But will you believe in God when there is no reason that you should because you haven't been blessed? For faith to be faith, you believe in God even when there is no corresponding evidence. 'Now faith is being sure of what we hope for and certain of what we do not see' (Hebrews 11:1).

Therefore the nearest you get to the answer to the question 'Why does God allow evil?' is: so that we might believe. For example, the only people that will be saved are those who believe.

> *For since in the wisdom of God the*
> *world through its wisdom did not*
> *know him, God was pleased through*
> *the foolishness of what was preached*
> *to save those who believe.*
>
> > *(1 Corinthians 1:21)*

It is a great privilege to believe, because there will be a day when *every* eye shall see him.

> *Look, he is coming with the clouds,*
> *and every eye will see him, even those*

*who pierced him; and all the peoples
of the earth will mourn because of
him. So shall it be! Amen.*

        (Revelation 1:7)

They will be *seeing* then. But that will not be
faith. Seeing and then 'believing' is not true faith.

Take Romans 8:28 (AV): 'And we know
that all things work together for good to
them that love God, to them who are the
called according to *his* purpose', which applies
only to Christians. I believe everything that
happens in the world is with a purpose, that
God allows things to happen and there is a
reason for it. But only the Christian has the
assurance that 'all things work together for
good'. You may say, 'It will all turn out well'.

Only to the saved is there such hope. All things work together for good for them that *love God*. To them who are the called according to his purpose. And so if you don't love God – surprise, surprise – this verse will never make sense. It cannot. This is a promise for members of the family only. It is the family secret. Those outside the family can never make sense of a verse like Romans 8:28; they cannot claim that promise.

One day, however, God will clear his name – openly. But those who clear his name now can say with Job, 'Though he slay me, yet will I hope in him' (Job 13:15). They are the ones who will stand proud in that day when everybody sees that the God of the Bible is a God of faithfulness, that he is just and righteous.

The second issue to address is: Why did they do it – these suicide bombers? Why would a human being want to bring such suffering on the world? What did they hope to accomplish? Are they driven by a perverse quest for significance? Are they driven by a theological conviction that they will go straight to heaven and be given sexual pleasures? Do they think this will make Allah look good in the world and win converts to Islam? The only answer is, sadly, that the events of 11 September have no natural or rational explanation. They were demonic.

The third issue: How did it happen? What caused it? For one thing, this should dispel any notion of the goodness of humankind. The most laughable statement anybody could make now is that human beings are 'basically good'. Nothing that has happened should surprise any Christian because the Bible said it in advance. Even for the Christian, the person who is saved, Jeremiah 17:9 describes my heart and yours: 'The heart is deceitful above all things and beyond cure. Who can understand it?' But the apostle Paul describes the unregenerate like this:

> *As it is written: 'There is no-one right-eous, not even one; there is no-one who understands, no-one who seeks God. All have turned away, they have together become worthless; there is no-one who does good, not even one. Their throats are open graves; their tongues practise deceit. The poison*

> *of vipers is on their lips. Their mouths*
> *are full of cursing and bitterness.*
> *Their feet are swift to shed blood; ruin*
> *and misery mark their ways, and the*
> *way of peace they do not know. There*
> *is no fear of God before their eyes.'*
> *(Romans 3:10–18)*

This shows what theologians have always called 'the doctrine of total depravity'. At the end of the day there are two explanations for the events of 11 September 2001: first, the sinfulness of humankind and, second, the hatred in a person that the devil exploits. Only people demon-possessed a thousand times over could do what these people did. In a word: it is *sin plus Satan*. For example, how could Judas Iscariot do what he did when he betrayed Jesus? He couldn't have done it by himself. The answer is: Satan prompted him (John 13:2). Then Judas did it.

I have to tell you that the devil who prompts people of hate today is the same 'god of this world' that will keep you blind if you are not yet saved. You may think that the devil will make an exception in your case; that you can enjoy the pleasures of sin for a season and one day you'll automatically get right with God on your own. The truth is, Satan will keep you blind. He hates you with an icy hatred and will keep you blind to Jesus Christ and his atoning sacrifice in order for your soul to be damned. Satan looks to and fro over the earth in order to enter somebody, and let me tell you who he most easily enters. Those who cannot forgive.

Therefore the devil exploits those who hold grudges and who say that 'What I've been through is so awful I can *never* forgive them'. Be careful, because then and there you invite Satan to come in, as my book *Total Forgiveness* shows. The most dangerous thing in the world is an unforgiving spirit. Could it be that God will use this very message to catch you in the nick of time if you are struggling with bitterness? One could no doubt sympathise with what you've had to go through. But we've all got a story to tell. And if we don't *totally forgive* we give Satan access to our hearts. What happened in New York and Washington could happen any moment, here or in other places. It is as a result of hate inviting Satan in, and the result is monstrous.

The fourth issue is: What spiritual change will there be in us? On 11 September 2001 the world changed. But was it a day that changed you? Maybe you were affected for a moment but after two or three days you just forgot about it. I heard of one head of a public school who happened to be in New York and who said that he did nothing but drink alcohol for three days. Are you are hoping time will cause the pain to go away? I know there is a danger of the foxhole conversion – General McArthur said there are no atheists in fox-holes (trenches). But listen. Strike while the iron is hot, if God has given this wake-up call to save you. My wife's brother-in-law – for whom people have been praying for forty-one years – was a backslider, but on the

Sunday following 11 September, to everyone's amazement, he went forward in a church and gave his heart back to the Lord.

Perhaps that can happen to somebody who reads these lines. You say you are upset about recent days. But what have they done to you? Will you go right back to the gutter of bitterness and fault-finding and pointing the finger? Or will this event mellow you, warm your heart and change you? What spiritual change has come over you? Could it be that one of the purposes for which God has allowed this tragedy is to give a wake-up call to those who are still alive?

One American church leader said that the events of 11 September are God's judgment on the United States for forgetting God – for the abortions, for the promiscuity. That may be the case, but retributive judgment is almost certainly only part of the picture. I happen to believe it is equally God's *gracious* judgment, to you and me. If we are still alive and we admit that we too could be killed by terrorism but are alive, the big question is: Are we ready to meet God? Be thankful that it is his gracious judgment.

What else do these issues imply? I think there are four implications. First, there are *ethical* implications. How do we treat our neighbours? And how do we treat Muslims? Is it our duty to retaliate? Is it the duty of a nation to retaliate? Is there one rule for the Christian and another for the State? There may be. But as a Christian, do I pray for my enemy? As a politician, do I seek to get even? I believe there are some answers. We must lower our voices and get over the need to see that certain people get caught and are brought to justice. Let us put it differently. The first principle is that we must love all Muslims and pray for them. And when you pray for them, you are praying that God will *bless* them. Whether or not this is a concept they hold to does not matter. 'A man convinced against his will is of the same opinion still.' It won't do to put a pistol to the head of anybody and say: 'Start changing.' The *heart* must be changed first. One must be mellowed inside. And nothing will convince such people like seeing our unfeigned love for them.

The next principle to remember is that most Muslims regret what has happened in recent days. Don't say that all Muslims are the same. After all, I can think of certain Christian leaders who make me blush. For if the Christian faith is to be judged by certain people, who would ever want to be a Christian? For not all Christians are the same.

A third principle is best summed up in the words of Dr Henry Kissinger: 'It is not retaliation that should be sought, but simply the end of terrorism.' We must keep that valid distinction in mind. It is not vengeance one must seek but the end of terrorism. Vengeance belongs to God, not us. 'Do not take revenge, my friends, but leave room for God's wrath, for it is written: "It is mine to avenge; I will repay," says the Lord' (Romans 12:19).

There are clear *eschatological* implications. Either we are in the very last days or we are not. I believe we are. I cannot say to you that it has been revealed to me as it was to Simeon that I would see the Lord in my day. Simeon was an old man and still believed that before he died he would see the Messiah. God had revealed such to him by the Holy Spirit (Luke 2:25–6). And then he saw Jesus. He said, 'Now I am ready to die.' But I cannot say that that has happened to me, that I will be alive when the Lord comes. But I will tell you right now, I will not be surprised if I am. I think the time is very, very short.

I believe that what happened on 11 September is the *beginning of the end*. I have consulted a variety of gifted scholars and seasoned prophetic people. Dr Paul Cain concurs: 'It's the beginning of the end.' Dr Billy Ball said to me: 'It is the beginning of the end.' Dr Ball has made a life study of eschatology. He has lived in the parables and the book of Revelation and he said to me that there is no doubt in his mind that what happened on 11 September is *the announcement of the midnight cry:* behold, the bridegroom comes, go out to meet him (see Matthew 25:6). And I believe that the cataclysmic day of 11 September 2001 has set in motion a definite sequence of events to be unfolded in these very last days.

In a word: Jesus is coming very soon. Lift up your heads, your redemption draws nigh! How does it make you feel? Well, there's that in all of us that makes us want life to go on as it was. I had looked forward to fishing and some retirement like others get when they reach my age. But it's as though God sent an angel to tap me on the shoulder, who said, 'R. T., sorry about this.' What if you were told by Michael the archangel that Jesus is coming this very day, how would it make you feel? Would you cry out in terror? Or could you say with John, 'even so, come Lord Jesus'?

I have to say furthermore that there are what I must call *eternal* implications. There are people in heaven today because of the event of 11 September. And – it is so sad – there are people in hell today because of 11 September. I was contacted in Key Largo by Premier Radio a day or so after it happened. Cindy Kent interviewed me live, transatlantic. She wanted my reaction and among other things, I said 'Do you realise that there are people now in hell? They did not wake up expecting this would be their last day.' It is a reminder that life at its longest is still short. It would not be a pretty sight or lovely sound if a video survived of what was happening on the plane that fell near Pittsburgh. You can be sure that they were unashamedly crying out to God. And I believe God heard their prayers. 'Everyone who calls on the name of the Lord will be saved' (Romans 10:13), and I doubt not that dozens called on the name of the Lord. God is merciful. But what about those in the twin towers who did not even have a second's warning?

There is a parallel between the second coming and what happened on 11 September. Let me explain what I mean by that. Jesus said that his second coming will come like a thief.

So you also must be ready, because the Son of Man will come at an hour when you do not expect him.

(Matthew 24:44)

But the day of the Lord will come like a thief. The heavens will disappear with a roar; the elements will be destroyed by fire, and the earth and everything in it will be laid bare.

(2 Peter 3:10)

Dr Billy Ball spoke in Westminster Chapel a number of years ago and actually said, 'There will be nuclear war.'

'Oh, no', different ones said, 'that cannot happen.'

He said, 'It will happen.'

We will see. But I know this, we are living in days in which – whatever else is true – you had better be sure that you know you will be saved. It will not matter whether certain people are 'brought to justice'. What about your soul? You have a soul. It is your only soul. No one else can answer for you.

There are, finally, *evangelistic* implications. Do *you* know for sure if you were to die today, you would go to heaven? Do you? If you stood before God – and one day you will, and he were to ask you (which he could do), 'Why should I let you into my heaven?', what would you say? I would urge you right now to hear these words. Two thousand years ago God sent his one and only son into the world. He was born of a virgin, which the Koran teaches. A Muslim who had been converted to Christ said to me that if you want to put a Muslim on the spot, get them to see the implications of the virgin birth of Jesus because Muslims are supposed to believe that. A logical conclusion, if they thought it through, would be that Jesus had no earthly father. Only the Holy Spirit could do what Luke 1:35 says happened:

> *The angel answered, 'The Holy Spirit will come upon you, and the power of the Most High will overshadow you. So the holy one to be born will be called the Son of God.'*

Jesus was and is the God-man. He died on a cross. What appeared at first to be the greatest tragedy in human history turned out to be the greatest event and the most glorious thing God ever did. It was the best kept secret from the foundation of the world that God was going to send his Son to die on a cross for our sins. I say to you, the reader, call on him because you need to be saved. Not because you need grace to get through the day. Call on him because there is a heaven and there is a hell, not because you just want to be able to manage and make sure you have a job. Transfer the trust that you have had in your good works to what Jesus did for you on the cross. Then one can see in your case that what happened on 11 September 200 is already beginning to work together for good.

In Revelation 10 the voice spoke to John and said, 'Take the scroll and eat it. It will turn your stomach sour, but in your mouth it will be as sweet as honey.' And so he did. 'I took it. I ate it. In my mouth it was sweet as honey.' And that's the good news, to think that something so stupendous is coming; the glory of the Lord will be manifested. You are going to see extraordinary things. 'But when I ate it my stomach turned sour.' You will also see extraordinary things that get worse. It will get much worse. And all this is described in the book of Revelation. You should begin to read it. It should not catch us by surprise.

Let me tell you what's going to happen down the road. I hope I'm alive to see it. I'm wouldn't be surprised if I am. Something will happen that – at long last – will get the attention of Jews all over the world and the Israelis. They are going to turn to the Lord. It's happening already secretly in Israel today. There are a surprising number of people in Israel being converted to Christ. But one day something will happen and it will spread like wildfire. Then you're going to find Israelis saying what no one ever dreamed they would say. They will look at the Muslims and say, 'Is it the temple mount you want? Take it. You can have it. We've got something better.' Because what happened two thousand years ago will have been revealed to them.

I don't mean to be unfair, but there are even some Christians who think, 'We've got to have the temple built.'

Nonsense! We are the temples of the Holy Ghost (1 Corinthians 6:19). The sacrifice of

45

Jesus caused the veil of the temple to be split from top to bottom (Matthew 27:51). When Israelis see the true Messiah, and grasp all this about the temple, they will say to Muslims: 'Take it. You can have it, we've got something better than that.'

Let it not surprise you that Muslims, right, left and centre, will say, 'We never thought we would see the day you would say that we could have the temple and the temple mount.' They are going to want what the converted Jews have. 'You've got something we don't have', they will say to Jews.

The day will therefore come when what seemed to be so important – the temple in Jerusalem, the very reason for all the trouble – will become an irrelevance. Because John said,

*I saw the Holy City, the new Jerusalem,
coming down out of heaven from God,
prepared as a bride beautifully dressed
for her husband. And I heard a loud
voice from the throne saying, 'Now the
dwelling of God is with men, and he
will live with them. They will be his
people, and God himself will be with
them and be their God. He will wipe
every tear from their eyes. There will
be no more death or mourning or
crying or pain, for the old order of
things has passed away.'*

*He who was seated on the throne
said, 'I am making everything new!'
Then he said, 'Write this down, for
these words are trustworthy and true.'*

(Revelation 21:2–5)

47

And that is what we are looking forward to. This present world is not all there is. We need to discern the signs of the times. If you will forgive the expression, 'You ain't seen nothing yet', because things will get simultaneously worse and better.

Abide with me: fast falls the eventide;
The darkness deepens; Lord, with me abide!
When other helpers fail, and comforts flee,
Help of the helpless, O abide with me.

Swift to its close ebbs out life's little day;
Earth's joys grow dim, its glories pass
    away;
Change and decay in all around I see:
O Thou who changest not, abide with me.

I need Thy presence every passing hour;
What but Thy grace can foil the tempter's
    power?
Who like Thyself my guide and stay can
    be?
Through cloud and sunshine, Lord, abide
    with me.

I fear no foe, with Thee at hand to bless;
Ills have no weight, and, tears no bitterness:
Where is death's sting? Where, grave, thy
    victory?
I triumph still, if Thou abide with me.

Hold Thou Thy cross before my closing
    eyes;
Shine through the gloom, and point me to
    the skies;

Heaven's morning breaks, and earth's vain
   shadows flee:
In life, in death, O Lord, abide with me.

HENRY FRANCIS LYTE, 1793–1847

This is the world
You loved so much that for it
You gave your only begotten
Son, our Lord and Saviour Jesus Christ, to
   hang
From the cross, done to death
Love nearly overwhelmed by hate
Light nearly extinguished by darkness
Life nearly destroyed by death –
But not quite –

For love vanquished hate
For life overcame death, there –
Light overwhelmed
Darkness, there –
And we can live with hope.
For peace,
For transfiguration, for compassion,
    for soldiers,
For civilians, for peace, for Shalom,
For family, for togetherness –

O my God, our God, O my Father
When will we ever learn?
When will they ever learn?

DESMOND TUTU*

*From *Great Christian Prayers*, ed. Louise and R. T. Kendall
(Hodder & Stoughton, 2000) p. 236.

The world changed on 11 September 2001.
Have you changed?

2

WANTED:
A NEW KIND OF HERO

So he said he would destroy them –
had not Moses, his chosen one, stood
in the breach before him to keep his
wrath from destroying them.
                    (Psalm 106:23)

I looked for a man among them
who would build up the wall and
stand before me in the gap on behalf
of the land so that I would not have

to destroy it, but I found none.
              (Ezekiel 22:30)

We are now in a new kind of war, yes, but perhaps it is not so new when you remember that many years ago the apostle Paul said,

> *Our struggle is not against flesh and blood, but against the rulers, against the authorities, against the powers of this dark world and against the spiritual forces of evil in the heavenly realms.*
>   *(Ephesians 6:12)*

President Bush says that what has happened recently shows 'a new kind of evil', but what is needed at a time like this is a new kind of hero. The world is looking for a hero. What is needed is someone who will stand in the gap and who will do a certain kind of praying.

First, *gracious* praying. You notice that the psalmist said, 'I would have destroyed them, had not Moses stood in the *gap* to keep the wrath of God from destroying them.' The secret to Moses' anointing and greatness was that he prayed for those who opposed his leadership. God looked down at Moses and said to him, 'These are a sorry lot that you've got. Do you know what I am going to do? I am going to destroy them and start all over with you' (see Numbers 14:12).

How would you feel if God said he was

going to do that with those who oppose you? I can remember some years ago that, if God had said to me, 'R. T., I know you've got a tough row to hoe – it's really hard – and I want you to know that up in heaven we see what you're going through and we're just going to eliminate all your opposition', I think I might have said, 'Thank you, Lord. Glory to God.' But do you know what Moses did? He said to the Lord, 'No, forgive them' (see Numbers 14:13–19).

That is *gracious* praying. And in a time when people cry out for retaliation and vengeance we have an almost unprecedented opportunity to show an exceedingly rare quality – it is called 'total forgiveness'. When we begin to pray for those involved in crime, instead of attacking them and saying, 'What's

the matter with these people?' we can pray
for them. We need to pray for those who are
infected with racial hatred, for those involved
in pornography, in prostitution, in drugs, and
for those who disregard the sanctity of human
life. After all Jesus made it so clear.

> *But I tell you who hear me: Love your
> enemies, do good to those who hate
> you, bless those who curse you, pray
> for those who ill-treat you. If someone
> strikes you on one cheek, turn to him
> the other also. If someone takes your
> cloak, do not stop him from taking
> your tunic. Give to everyone who asks
> you, and if anyone takes what belongs
> to you, do not demand it back. Do to*

> *others as you would have them do to*
> *you.*
>
> *(Luke 6:27–31)*

I can imagine that many centuries ago, when Saul of Tarsus was doing everything to eradicate Christianity, the angels perhaps came along and said to God, 'What are we going to do about this Saul of Tarsus? Shall we go down and just wipe him out?' And God may have said, 'There are people praying for him. Do you know what I am going to do? I think I'll just save him. And make him a sovereign vessel.' I wonder how many were really praying for Saul of Tarsus then? And how many people are praying for Osama Bin Laden at this particular time?

There are stories coming out of the Middle East of Muslims who, in their dreams, are seeing that Jesus is the Son of God, and that he died on the cross.

God moves in a mysterious way
His wonders to perform;
He plants his footsteps in the sea,
And rides upon the storm.

WILLIAM COWPER, 1731–1800

With God, all things are possible. Let us pray that God will do what eye has not seen, nor ear heard, what most people cannot even imagine would happen. If John Wesley was right when he said, 'God does nothing but in answer to prayer', then somebody must have prayed for Saul of Tarsus, the most unlikely person to be converted.

But how do we pray for our leaders? I answer very simply – in eight words: *Wisdom and courage to show justice and mercy.* The new kind of hero that is needed, then, is one who will spend time in *gracious* praying.

Second, *anonymous* praying. What is needed today is the kind of hero who will quietly intercede, who will stand in the gap and then keep quiet about it. Many years ago I read a little pamphlet entitled, 'Where are the intercessors?' Intercession is an enterprise that has almost perished from the earth. What is needed is anonymous intercession, however; interceding without broadcasting it. Jesus called it 'not letting your right hand know what your left hand is doing'.

I don't want to be unfair, but it seems to me that too many people who want to engage in intercession want to solve the problem, rather than just pray. For example, the last thing Sir John Stevens needs is for a thousand people to phone him at New Scotland Yard and say, 'I have a word from the Lord for Sir John.' Sometimes I dread sharing a problem with others for prayer, because almost every time they'll come to me within a week or two and say, 'I know what you should do.' I didn't ask them to give me a word! I just wanted them to pray. Just to pray.

We need those who will intercede with a low profile and with no profile. I suppose that if Billy Graham sent out a letter stating that all who pledged to pray for him every day could be his personal guest in Montreat, North Carolina, once a year, he would get ten million volunteers. How many are willing to pray for those they will never meet, never have a phone call from and never receive a letter from, but are prepared to wait until they get to heaven? Therefore, this new kind of hero will engage in *anonymous* praying.

Third, *passionate* praying. I want to give you this little acrostic to illustrate how we stand in the gap: GAP – Gracious praying, Anonymous praying, Passionate praying.

There are two kinds of praying in this connection. We can read a prayer and there is nothing wrong with that. (My wife and I have come up with a book, which is a collection of prayers of great Christians over the centuries, especially for people to read.) You can also work through a prayer list every day.

But the kind of praying I'm talking about is praying with tears. Do you know the first time the word 'tears' appears in the Bible? It is in 2 Kings 20:5 after Hezekiah had been told his time was up. He wept before the Lord and cried out to God and Isaiah came back to him and said, 'This is what the LORD, the God of your father David, says: I have heard your prayer and seen your tears.'

Try tears. That is *passionate* praying. My wife Louise will never forget the time Rodney and Adonica Howard-Browne prayed for her and she was instantly healed. Louise happened to look up at Adonica and saw that tears were rolling down her cheeks as she prayed.

This is such an hour – if it does not drive

us to our knees, or to tears – what will? And the kind of praying that is needed now is gracious praying, anonymous praying, passionate praying.

Perhaps God has got the attention of the world in recent days, and no doubt some are praying as they haven't done in years.

But now, paradoxical as it may seem, we need to get God's attention! Try tears. So the next time you're riding in the tube and you hear the words 'Mind the gap' remember: Stand in the gap, stand in the gap, pray, pray, pray; gracious praying, anonymous praying, passionate praying. Accept the call to be a new kind of hero, such as the world has not seen; to stand in the gap.

Heavenly Father, do please take this message; may it make a difference in our private lives. May we take the words of Jesus seriously, that we will not be like those who pray only in order to be seen, who give only when it's recognised, but that we will learn to go behind closed doors and accept the promise that our Father who sees what is done in secret will reward us. Raise up a new breed of Christians, a generation of gracious, anonymous and passionate intercessors that will change the world. We pray in Jesus' name. Amen.

R. T. Kendall

Total Forgiveness
Achieving God's greatest challenge

Answering God's challenging call for
Total Forgiveness may be the hardest thing
we ever have to do.

*'If I could have only one of R. T.'s books,
this would be my choice. There is no more
important message for the Church today.'*
Rob Parsons

0 340 75639X

R. T. Kendall

The Sensitivity of the Spirit

It is easy to imagine we are living in the immediate power of the Holy Spirit, especially if our lives are comfortable and going just as we would wish them to. But the Holy Spirit will follow his own path and, if we are not prepared to go with him, will move on without us.

*'Will help every Christian experience
peace and calm.'*
David Yonggi Cho

0 340 75628 4

R. T. Kendall

The Thorn in the Flesh

Many of us will know what it is like to be afflicted with a 'thorn in the flesh', a painful and chronic problem which does not seem to go away. R.T. explains how it can actually lead us into unimaginable intimacy with Jesus.

'Hope for all who struggle
with impossible conditions.'
Steve Chalke

0 340 74546 0

R. T. Kendall

The Anointing
Yesterday, today, tomorrow

Are you frustrated that your gift has not
been recognised? Your moment will come!
R.T. Kendall helps each of us to discover
the anointing of the Holy Spirit and
God's unique plan for our lives.

'Utterly compelling.'
Rob Parsons

0 340 72144 8

Compiled by Louise and R. T. Kendall

Great Christian Prayers

*From the rich history of Christian faith –
a prayer for every day of the year*

From St Augustine and St Basil to Mother Teresa
and Billy Graham, this unique anthology of
prayers spans not only the years but also the rich
diversity of Christian tradition.

'It's like eavesdropping on conversations with God!'
Sir Cliff Richard

0 340 78583 7

R T Kendall

In Pursuit of His Glory
My 25 years at Westminster Chapel

Published to mark his retirement,
a revealing, moving and inspirational account
of R.T. Kendall's eventful and occasionally
turbulent 25-year tenure as Minister
of Westminster Chapel.

0 340 78647 7

Published in February 2002